From Shirley Stutzman

W9-CFA-130

Quilt Art
'88

Engagement Calendar

*A collection of prize-winning
quilts from across the country.*

Another quality product from your *American Quilter's Society*.

Color photography by Donahue Studios, Inc., Evansville, Indiana.

American Quilter's Society

P.O. Box 3290 • Paducah, Kentucky 42001

On the cover:

ROSES ON THE CABIN by Joanne Holzknecht, Brooklyn Center, Minnesota. 85″ x 85″. Appliqued roses add a touch of elegance to an old classic. The symmetric center and asymmetric corners bring this quilt out of the ordinary. It won a double award at the Minnesota Quilter's, Inc. Show, "Quilting by the River".

Printed and Bound in Hong Kong
by Everbest Printing Co., Ltd.
Four Colour Imports, Ltd., Louisville.

Quilt Art '88

Klaudeen Hansen

Annette Riddle

This is the fourth year for the *Quilt Art* engagement calendar published by the American Quilter's Society. Once again, Klaudeen Hansen of Sun Prairie, Wisconsin and Annette Riddle of Marshall, Wisconsin have done an excellent job of finding the top quilts in the country. Klaudeen and Annette selected the quilts in *Quilt Art '88* on the basis of excellent workmanship, color and design. If you have been to one of the major quilt shows recently, chances are you've seen some of these quilts in person! The name of each quilt artist, her home town, the size of her quilt and a few facts about the quilt are given. Not enough can be said about the women (and some men) who have made quilting the art form it is today. As you carefully study each full-color photograph in this calendar, try to appreciate the hours the maker spent on her quilt—the hours designing it, the piecing, the quilting, the special touches. The map below indicates where each quiltmaker lives who has a quilt featured in *Quilt Art '88*. There is also a quilt from Alaska—54 in all for you to enjoy in 1988!

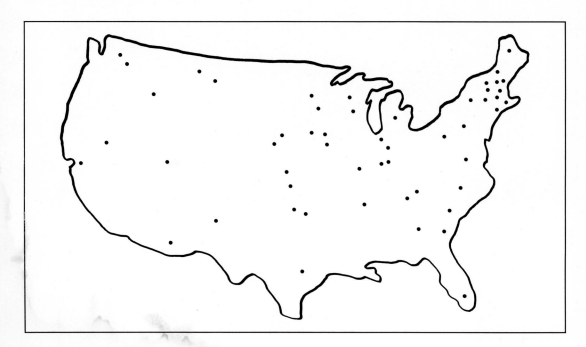

DECEMBER / JANUARY *1999*

MONDAY
28

TUESDAY
29

WEDNESDAY
30

THURSDAY
31

FRIDAY   NEW YEAR'S DAY
1

MT. SHUKSAN-SHALOM by Karen Schoepflin Hagen, Richland, Washington. 86″ x 96″. Mt. Shuksan reflects into wind-ruffled Picture Lake, North Cascades National Park in Washington State. The frame repeats colors of the mountain, the trees and the reflection idea. Each corner of the frame offers a close-up of the evergreen trees of the area. "Shalom" means peace and harmony.

SATURDAY
2
(Dave Hall
(Kase Haus manager)
Blue rm.

SUNDAY
3

JANUARY						
S	M	T	W	T	F	S
					1	2
3	4	5	6	7	8	9
10	11	12	13	14	15	16
17	18	19	20	21	22	23
24	25	26	27	28	29	30
31						

JANUARY

MONDAY
4

TUESDAY
5

WEDNESDAY
6

THURSDAY
7

FRIDAY
8

NOSEGAY by Judy Simmons, Coral Springs, Florida. 36″ round. Broderie Perse applique and stipple quilting were used to complete this delicate wall quilt. A hooked rug was its inspiration. It was a blue ribbon winner at the South Florida Fair and was displayed at the Sunset Quilt Show in Miami, Florida, and AQS Show in Paducah, Kentucky.

SATURDAY
9

SUNDAY
10

JANUARY						
S	**M**	**T**	**W**	**T**	**F**	**S**
					1	2
3	4	5	6	7	8	9
10	11	12	13	14	15	16
17	18	19	20	21	22	23
24	25	26	27	28	29	30
31						

JANUARY

MONDAY
11

TUESDAY
12

WEDNESDAY
13

THURSDAY
14

FRIDAY
15

HELLO HALLEY'S by Carol Anne Grotrian, Quincy, Massachusetts. 60″ x 60″. This quilt is machine and hand pieced and hand quilted. It is a scrap bag quilt using commercial prints and solids and hand-dyed solids. The border planets are air brushed and then reverse appliqued. Exhibited at the 1986 Vermont Quilt Festival.

SATURDAY
16

SUNDAY
17

JANUARY						
S	M	T	W	T	F	S
					1	2
3	4	5	6	7	8	9
10	11	12	13	14	15	16
17	18	19	20	21	22	23
24	25	26	27	28	29	30
31						

JANUARY

MONDAY   MARTIN LUTHER KING JR.'S BIRTHDAY OBSERVED
18

TUESDAY
19

WEDNESDAY
20

THURSDAY
21

FRIDAY
22

POOR BUTTERFLY by Dorothy S. Finley, Memphis, Tennessee. Broderie Perse applique, trapunto and stipple quilting are some of the techniques used to complete this large quilt. It required 2,475 hours to finish. It was a blue ribbon winner at the NQA Show, Decatur, Illinois, and at the Smoky Mountain Quilt Competition and Show, Oak Ridge, Tennessee.

SATURDAY
23

SUNDAY
24

JANUARY						
S	M	T	W	T	F	S
					1	2
3	4	5	6	7	8	9
10	11	12	13	14	15	16
17	18	19	20	21	22	23
24	25	26	27	28	29	30
31						

JANUARY

MONDAY
25

TUESDAY
26

WEDNESDAY
27

THURSDAY
28

FRIDAY
29

REDS AND VALLEYS by Georgia M. Springer, Raleigh, North Carolina. 24″ x 24″. This quilt was based on the traditional triangle template, exploring variations of that pattern using cut throughs, gradation of color and large patterned fabric. It was displayed at the Triangle Area Quilt Artists Show and Quilts From The Ohio Experience, a one-woman show.

SATURDAY
30

SUNDAY
31

JANUARY						
S	M	T	W	T	F	S
					1	2
3	4	5	6	7	8	9
10	11	12	13	14	15	16
17	18	19	20	21	22	23
24	25	26	27	28	29	30
31						

FEBRUARY

MONDAY

1

TUESDAY

2

WEDNESDAY

3

THURSDAY

4

FRIDAY

5

**"VALENTINE ROSE",
DOUBLE WEDDING
RING** by Linda Peterson,
Great Falls, Montana. 98″
x 108″. Appliqued roses
enhance this fine old
pattern made as an
anniversary gift for Linda's
parents. It won First Place
at the Western Heritage
Center Quilt Competition,
Billings, Montana.

SATURDAY

6

SUNDAY

7

Tom Patterson

FEBRUARY						
S	M	T	W	T	F	S
	1	2	3	4	5	6
7	8	9	10	11	12	13
14	15	16	17	18	19	20
21	22	23	24	25	26	27
28	29					

FEBRUARY

MONDAY
8

Tom Patterson
#25
no breakfast

TUESDAY
9

WEDNESDAY
10

THURSDAY
11

FRIDAY   LINCOLN'S BIRTHDAY
12   *Ligioner*
meet 12:50

VOICE OF FREEDOM by
Barbara Temple, Marietta,
Georgia. 66″ x 65″.
Barbara was so moved by
the Lincoln Memorial that
she designed this piece so
those feelings would not be
forgotten. It was juried
into the AQS Show,
Paducah, Kentucky.

SATURDAY
13

SUNDAY   ST. VALENTINE'S DAY
14

FEBRUARY

S	M	T	W	T	F	S
	1	2	3	4	5	6
7	8	9	10	11	12	13
14	15	16	17	18	19	20
21	22	23	24	25	26	27
28	29					

FEBRUARY

MONDAY   WASHINGTON'S BIRTHDAY OBSERVED
15

TUESDAY
16

WEDNESDAY   ASH WEDNESDAY
17

THURSDAY
18

FRIDAY
19

YORU no UMI (Night Flower) by Mihoko W. Tsong, Boise, Idaho. 86″ x 105″. Each block is a hand appliqued plum blossom design from Japanese family crests. Seven blocks were done by Mom's Quilters, who also contributed many hours of hand quilting. Displayed at "Pieces of our Lives" and Best of Show winner at the Western Idaho Fair.

SATURDAY
20

SUNDAY
21

FEBRUARY

S	M	T	W	T	F	S
	1	2	3	4	5	6
7	8	9	10	11	12	13
14	15	16	17	18	19	20
21	22	23	24	25	26	27
28	29					

FEBRUARY

MONDAY
22

TUESDAY
23

WEDNESDAY
24

THURSDAY
25

FRIDAY
26

WISCONSIN BARNS by Marge Etter, Lake Mills, Wisconsin. 72″ x 88″. The seven barns in this quilt were patterned after barns in the book *Barns of Wisconsin* by Jerry Apps and Allen Strong to record the vanishing barns in her state. The quilt won Viewer's Choice and First Place in Applique at the Fort Atkinson, Wisconsin Piecemakers Quilt Guild Show.

SATURDAY
27

SUNDAY
28

FEBRUARY						
S	M	T	W	T	F	S
	1	2	3	4	5	6
7	8	9	10	11	12	13
14	15	16	17	18	19	20
21	22	23	24	25	26	27
28	29					

FEBRUARY / MARCH

MONDAY
29

TUESDAY
1

WEDNESDAY
2

THURSDAY
3

FRIDAY
4

LILY GARDEN by
Catherine Byron, Concord,
Massachusetts. 89″ x 98″.
Outstanding choice of
quilting designs enhances
this adaptation of the
Carolina Lily pattern. It
has been shown at the New
England Images II,
Concord Piecemakers Quilt
Show and the Concord
Antiquarian Museum.

SATURDAY
5

SUNDAY
6

MARCH						
S	M	T	W	T	F	S
			1	2	3	4	5
6	7	8	9	10	11	12
13	14	15	16	17	18	19
20	21	22	23	24	25	26
27	28	29	30	31		

MARCH

MONDAY
7

TUESDAY
8

WEDNESDAY
9

THURSDAY
10

FRIDAY
11

SAMPLER IN THE ROUND by the Geechee Quilter's Guild, Savannah, Georgia. 76″ x 76″. This quilt was designed, assembled and quilted by Ronnie Durrence. Ruth Brown and Mary Weaver selected colors and fabrics. Others involved were Pearl Rains, Inez Banner, Veda Haselden, Bonnie Ricks, Linda Piatt, Laura Mayes, Ferma Jean Kirkpatrick and Quretha Bassett.

SATURDAY
12

SUNDAY
13

		MARCH				
S	M	T	W	T	F	S
		1	2	3	4	5
6	7	8	9	10	11	12
13	14	15	16	17	18	19
20	21	22	23	24	25	26
27	28	29	30	31		

MARCH

MONDAY
14

TUESDAY
15

WEDNESDAY
16

THURSDAY   ST. PATRICK'S DAY
17

FRIDAY
18

LILY IN THE SKY WITH DIAMONDS by Jennifer Amor, Columbia, South Carolina. 42″ x 42″. A number of ribbons has been collected with this precisely pieced quilt. ¼″ pieces are used to create the shaded three-dimensional effects.

SATURDAY
19

SUNDAY
20

MARCH						
S	M	T	W	T	F	S
		1	2	3	4	5
6	7	8	9	10	11	12
13	14	15	16	17	18	19
20	21	22	23	24	25	26
27	28	29	30	31		

MARCH

MONDAY
21

TUESDAY
22

WEDNESDAY
23

THURSDAY
24

FRIDAY
25

VENETIAN TILE by Suzanne Warren Brown, Arkansas City, Kansas. The medallion center and carefully planned piecing are equally as outstanding as the intricate quilting designs. The center is an adaptation of a venetian tile floor. It won the Sweepstakes Award at the Kansas State Fair.

SATURDAY
26 *27*

SUNDAY
27

2 rooms   *Elvie Miller Called 1-13*

4 people
Lynn Morris Band

MARCH						
S	M	T	W	T	F	S
		1	2	3	4	5
6	7	8	9	10	11	12
13	14	15	16	17	18	19
20	21	22	23	24	25	26
27	28	29	30	31		

MARCH / APRIL

SONG LILY by Merial S. Liberty, Irasburg, Vermont. 37″ round. The design for this unusual piece was taken from a book of Chinese designs. The "Song" in the title is the name of the dynasty. It was displayed by invitation at the Rutland, Vermont Quilt Show.

SATURDAY   PASSOVER
2

SUNDAY   EASTER
3

APRIL						
S	M	T	W	T	F	S
					1	2
3	4	5	6	7	8	9
10	11	12	13	14	15	16
17	18	19	20	21	22	23
24	25	26	27	28	29	30

APRIL

MONDAY
4

TUESDAY
5

WEDNESDAY
6

THURSDAY
7

FRIDAY
8

MARY'S GARDEN by Mary Rushing, Virginia Beach, Virginia. 103″ x 103″. Drafting and cutting patterns from library books completed the set of 25 applique blocks for this quilt. It was a prize winner at the Tidewater Quilter's Guild Show.

SATURDAY
9

SUNDAY
10

APRIL

S	M	T	W	T	F	S
					1	2
3	4	5	6	7	8	9
10	11	12	13	14	15	16
17	18	19	20	21	22	23
24	25	26	27	28	29	30

APRIL

MONDAY

11

TUESDAY

12

WEDNESDAY

13

THURSDAY

14

FRIDAY

15

NOAH'S ARK by Connie Oliver, Pittsburgh, Pennsylvania. 47½″ x 49½″. Hand applique, quilting, embroidery, painting and piecing celebrate the joy of God's creatures returning to dry land. It was juried into the AQS Show, Paducah, Kentucky.

SATURDAY

16

SUNDAY

17

APRIL

S	M	T	W	T	F	S
					1	2
3	4	5	6	7	8	9
10	11	12	13	14	15	16
17	18	19	20	21	22	23
24	25	26	27	28	29	30

APRIL

MONDAY
18

TUESDAY
19

WEDNESDAY
20

THURSDAY
21

FRIDAY
22

CINNAMON by Julia Overton Needham, Knoxville, Tennessee. 78″ x 90″. Adventurous use of a striped fabric was the 1st step in the creation of this variation on clamshell applique. It won a blue ribbon at the Smoky Mountain Quilt Show, Oak Ridge, Tennessee and was juried into the AQS Show, Paducah, Kentucky.

SATURDAY
23

SUNDAY
24

APRIL

S	M	T	W	T	F	S
					1	2
3	4	5	6	7	8	9
10	11	12	13	14	15	16
17	18	19	20	21	22	23
24	25	26	27	28	29	30

APRIL / MAY

MONDAY
25

TUESDAY
26

WEDNESDAY
27

THURSDAY
28

FRIDAY
29

CATHAY by Paulette Peters, Elkhorn, Nebraska. 84″ x 84″. Inspired by her husband's trip to China, Paulette researched and used Chinese decorative motifs. Colors were inspired by an antique Chinese screen. CATHAY was featured at Heritage Quilter's Show and was Viewer's Choice at the Cottonwood Quilter's Show.

SATURDAY
30

SUNDAY
1

			MAY			
S	M	T	W	T	F	S
1	2	3	4	5	6	7
8	9	10	11	12	13	14
15	16	17	18	19	20	21
22	23	24	25	26	27	28
29	30	31				

MAY

MONDAY

2

TUESDAY

3

WEDNESDAY

4

THURSDAY

5

FRIDAY

6

MOTHER'S FLOWER GARDEN: A TRIBUTE TO JOSEPHINE by Carol Hornback, Granite City, Illinois. 102″ x 112″. This beautifully appliqued quilt also contains some padding and trapunto. Fabrics are cotton and cotton/polyester blends. Carol just completed the quilt in time to be included in this calendar.

SATURDAY

7

SUNDAY   **MOTHER'S DAY**

8

MAY

S	M	T	W	T	F	S
1	2	3	4	5	6	7
8	9	10	11	12	13	14
15	16	17	18	19	20	21
22	23	24	25	26	27	28
29	30	31				

MAY

MONDAY
9

TUESDAY
10

WEDNESDAY
11

THURSDAY
12

FRIDAY
13

VIOLETS by Mary Jo McCabe, Davenport, Iowa. 82″ x 96″. The curved 2-patch system was used to create the center medallion nosegay of violets and the center border. It was juried into the AQS Show, Paducah, Kentucky.

SATURDAY
14

SUNDAY
15

MAY						
S	M	T	W	T	F	S
1	2	3	4	5	6	7
8	9	10	11	12	13	14
15	16	17	18	19	20	21
22	23	24	25	26	27	28
29	30	31				

MAY

MONDAY
16

TUESDAY
17

WEDNESDAY
18

THURSDAY
19

FRIDAY
20

MY FRIENDSHIP GARDEN by Hazel Potter, Reno, Nevada. Blocks for this quilt were made by friends in her Reno Quilt Club and family members. Hazel added the picket fence and the quilting, which includes rabbits, cats, quail, birds, butterflies and ivy in the sashing. It was one of three quilts included in the Sierra Arts Festival in Reno.

SATURDAY   **ARMED FORCES DAY**
21

SUNDAY
22

		MAY				
S	M	T	W	T	F	S
1	2	3	4	5	6	7
8	9	10	11	12	13	14
15	16	17	18	19	20	21
22	23	24	25	26	27	28
29	30	31				

MAY

MONDAY
23

TUESDAY
24

WEDNESDAY
25

THURSDAY
26

FRIDAY
27

KALEIDOSCOPE by Suzanne Coulter, Tucson, Arizona. 67½″ x 91″. Manipulation of the printed fabric provided the individuality of all 17 Castle Wall block centers. A first place winner at the Piece Conference and Viewer's Choice at the Quilter's Guild Show, both in Tucson.

SATURDAY
28

SUNDAY
29

		MAY				
S	M	T	W	T	F	S
1	2	3	4	5	6	7
8	9	10	11	12	13	14
15	16	17	18	19	20	21
22	23	24	25	26	27	28
29	30	31				

MAY / JUNE

MONDAY   MEMORIAL DAY
30

TUESDAY
31

WEDNESDAY
1

THURSDAY
2

FRIDAY
3

WIND ROSE by Mazey Buckley, San Antonio, Texas. Mazey's husband's hobby was the inspiration for this very personal wall quilt. Old marine maps called the compass design the "wind rose". It has hung at the Brigham Young University Art Gallery and Crossroads of the American West in Utah.

SATURDAY
4

SUNDAY
5

			JUNE			
S	M	T	W	T	F	S
			1	2	3	4
5	6	7	8	9	10	11
12	13	14	15	16	17	18
19	20	21	22	23	24	25
26	27	28	29	30		

JUNE

MONDAY
6

TUESDAY
7

WEDNESDAY
8

THURSDAY
9

FRIDAY
10

SPIRIT by Catherine Anthony, Houston, Texas. 72″ x 72″ x 72″. This hand pieced and hand quilted piece is part of a series about women that Catherine admires. This particular one is a tribute to the spirit of Dominque DeMenil, who exposed Houston to good contemporary art against all odds.

SATURDAY
11

SUNDAY
12

JUNE

S	M	T	W	T	F	S
			1	2	3	4
5	6	7	8	9	10	11
12	13	14	15	16	17	18
19	20	21	22	23	24	25
26	27	28	29	30		

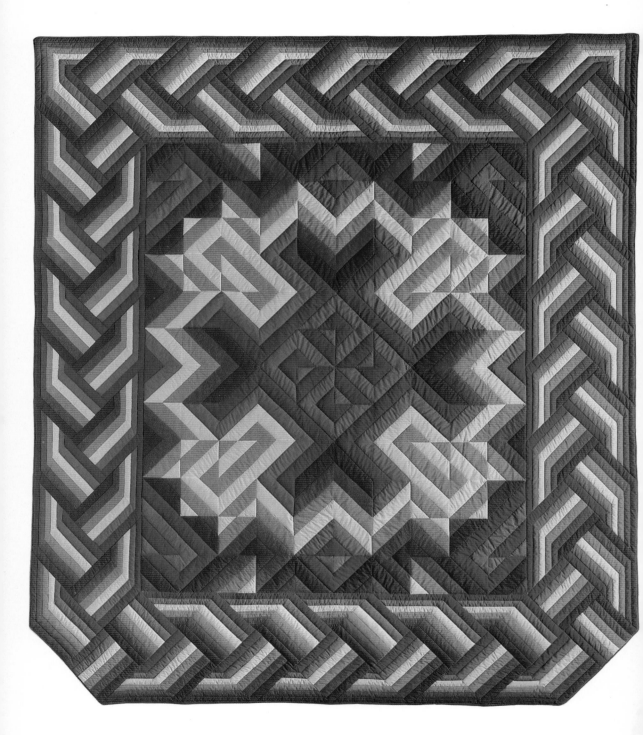

JUNE

MONDAY
13

TUESDAY **FLAG DAY**
14

WEDNESDAY
15

THURSDAY
16

FRIDAY
17

KING'S X by John Flynn, Billings, Montana. 108″ x 124″. This quilt is a variation of the Governor's Palace Maze pattern with a braided rainbow border of his own design. A People's Choice Award was won at the Western Heritage Center in Billings, and the quilt was shown at the Quilter's Art Guild Show in the Museum of the Rockies, Bozeman, Montana.

SATURDAY
18
19

4 person   *Elvie called*
1-13
2rms
Harmonious Wail

SUNDAY **FATHER'S DAY**
19

			JUNE			
S	M	T	W	T	F	S
				1	2	3	4
5	6	7	8	9	10	11
12	13	14	15	16	17	18
19	20	21	22	23	24	25
26	27	28	29	30		

JUNE

MONDAY
20

TUESDAY
21

WEDNESDAY
22

THURSDAY
23

FRIDAY
24

JAN'S FAN by Janet J. Ratner, Wantagh, New York. 82″ x 82″. Jan took the original Grandmother's Fan pattern and lifted it up off the corner to make it more fan-like. Then she embellished it with every sewing and embroidery technique she knew. It has been exhibited at the Long Island Fair, World of Quilts and Long Island Quilter's Convention, New York.

SATURDAY
25

SUNDAY
26

			JUNE			
S	M	T	W	T	F	S
				1	2	3	4
5	6	7	8	9	10	11
12	13	14	15	16	17	18
19	20	21	22	23	24	25
26	27	28	29	30		

JUNE / JULY

MONDAY

27

TUESDAY

28

WEDNESDAY

29

THURSDAY

30

FRIDAY

1

LOVE IN THE STARS by
Tami Marshall, Rockford,
Washington. 91½″ x 91½″.
Finely quilted feathers
have put this quilt in the
winner's circle many times.
It has won Best of Show at
the Washington State
Grange Competition, the
Washington Interstate Fair
and the Western Heritage
Center, Billings, Montana.

SATURDAY

2

SUNDAY

3

		JULY				
S	M	T	W	T	F	S
					1	2
3	4	5	6	7	8	9
10	11	12	13	14	15	16
17	18	19	20	21	22	23
24	25	26	27	28	29	30
31						

JULY

MONDAY   INDEPENDENCE DAY

4

TUESDAY

5

WEDNESDAY

6

THURSDAY

7

FRIDAY

8

VERMONT SAMPLER by
Nanine Hutchinson, East
Thetford, Vermont. 70″ x
106″. Forty different blocks
explore a variety of
techniques. It was
displayed at Vermont Quilt
Festival, New England
Images II and Northern
Lights Quilting Guild
Show.

SATURDAY

9

SUNDAY

10

			JULY			
S	M	T	W	T	F	S
					1	2
3	4	5	6	7	8	9
10	11	12	13	14	15	16
17	18	19	20	21	22	23
24	25	26	27	28	29	30
31						

JULY

MONDAY

11

TUESDAY

12

WEDNESDAY

13

THURSDAY

14

FRIDAY

15

RRIII - BIRD QUILT by Diane Phillips Caton, Marion, Iowa. 57″ x 75″. "This original design is part of an ongoing series of quilts expressing my reaction to the loss of my mother." Displayed at NQA, Decatur, Illinois and juried into AQS Show, Paducah, Kentucky and the University of Iowa Project Art.

SATURDAY

16

SUNDAY

17

JULY						
S	M	T	W	T	F	S
					1	2
3	4	5	6	7	8	9
10	11	12	13	14	15	16
17	18	19	20	21	22	23
24	25	26	27	28	29	30
31						

JULY

MONDAY
18

TUESDAY
19

WEDNESDAY
20

THURSDAY
21

FRIDAY
22

BIRD OF PARADISE by Mary R. Johnson, Munster, Indiana. 92″ x 78½″. Years of avid fabric collecting made possible the unique feel of this hand appliqued and hand quilted piece. It was completed just in time to be included in this edition of the calendar.

SATURDAY
23

SUNDAY
24

JULY						
S	M	T	W	T	F	S
					1	2
3	4	5	6	7	8	9
10	11	12	13	14	15	16
17	18	19	20	21	22	23
24	25	26	27	28	29	30
31						

JULY

MONDAY
25

TUESDAY
26

WEDNESDAY
27

THURSDAY
28

FRIDAY
29

PINE TREES AND TULIPS by Linda S. Consolini, Bedford, New Hampshire. 85″ x 105″. This quilt made its debut at New England Images II, Topsfield, Massachusetts. The graceful tulips provide a focal point for this medallion within a medallion. The unifying force is the network of fine grid quilting enlivened with hearts and tulips.

SATURDAY
30

SUNDAY
31

		JULY				
S	M	T	W	T	F	S
					1	2
3	4	5	6	7	8	9
10	11	12	13	14	15	16
17	18	19	20	21	22	23
24	25	26	27	28	29	30
31						

AUGUST

MONDAY

1

TUESDAY

2

WEDNESDAY

3

THURSDAY

4

FRIDAY

5

BARGELLO III TAJ MAHAL by Margaret Mooney, Burlington, Massachusetts. The design is loosely based on Bargello needlepoint designs. Strip piecing was used plus some reverse applique. The color was achieved by using hand-dyed cotton. It was juried into New England Images II.

SATURDAY

6

SUNDAY

7

AUGUST						
S	M	T	W	T	F	S
	1	2	3	4	5	6
7	8	9	10	11	12	13
14	15	16	17	18	19	20
21	22	23	24	25	26	27
28	29	30	31			

AUGUST

MONDAY
8

TUESDAY
9

WEDNESDAY
10

THURSDAY
11

FRIDAY
12

SHADED GRAPES by Nathalie A. Chick, Wells, Maine. 80″ x 96″. More than two years were devoted to the fine hand applique and exquisite hand quilting in this quilt. It won Best of Show at Evergreen Quilt Show and New England Images II.

SATURDAY
13

SUNDAY
14

AUGUST

S	M	T	W	T	F	S
	1	2	3	4	5	6
7	8	9	10	11	12	13
14	15	16	17	18	19	20
21	22	23	24	25	26	27
28	29	30	31			

AUGUST

MONDAY
15

TUESDAY
16

WEDNESDAY
17

THURSDAY
18

FRIDAY
19

CLAMS CASINO by Dianne Duncan Thomas, Omaha, Nebraska. 76″ x 76″. Ideas gleaned from a magazine article about a California quilter came together in this three-dimensional wall quilt. Multiple ribbons were won at Omaha Quilter's Spring Show, Exhibit Fort Omaha and Nevada State Fair.

SATURDAY
20

SUNDAY
21

AUGUST						
S	M	T	W	T	F	S
	1	2	3	4	5	6
7	8	9	10	11	12	13
14	15	16	17	18	19	20
21	22	23	24	25	26	27
28	29	30	31			

AUGUST

MONDAY
22

TUESDAY
23

WEDNESDAY
24

THURSDAY
25

FRIDAY
26

RASPBERRY SHERBET by Lyn Piercy, San Francisco, California. 88″ x 101″. The stuffed work in the wide pink border was designed from the central motif. Quilting is diamonds in the middle and close diagonal lines in the darker pink areas. The pieced flower designs are original. A multiple winner at the California State Fair and the Capitol City Quilt Festival, Sacramento, CA.

SATURDAY
27

SUNDAY
28

_						
AUGUST						
S	M	T	W	T	F	S
	1	2	3	4	5	6
7	8	9	10	11	12	13
14	15	16	17	18	19	20
21	22	23	24	25	26	27
28	29	30	31			

AUGUST / SEPTEMBER

MONDAY
29

TUESDAY
30

WEDNESDAY
31

THURSDAY
1

FRIDAY
2

UNTITLED SAMPLER by Gerry O'Neill, Oak Ridge, Tennessee. This quilt was made by the "quilt-as-you-go" method. It was a first place winner at the NQA Show in Bell Buckle, TN, and also won awards at the Smoky Mountain Quilt Show in Oak Ridge, TN, and the "La Fete de Piguage" in Baton Rouge, LA.

SATURDAY
3

SUNDAY
4

SEPTEMBER						
S	M	T	W	T	F	S
				1	2	3
4	5	6	7	8	9	10
11	12	13	14	15	16	17
18	19	20	21	22	23	24
25	26	27	28	29	30	

SEPTEMBER

MONDAY   LABOR DAY
5

TUESDAY
6

WEDNESDAY
7

THURSDAY
8

FRIDAY
9

ROSEMALING by Betty Ekern Suiter, Racine, Wisconsin. 40″ x 60″. Betty's Norwegian heritage inspired her to make this hand appliqued and hand quilted piece. It has won awards at the Prairie Heritage Quilt Guild Show, Sun Prairie, Wisconsin, NQA Show, Decatur, Illinois and the Wisconsin State Fair.

SATURDAY
10

SUNDAY
11

SEPTEMBER

S	M	T	W	T	F	S
				1	2	3
4	5	6	7	8	9	10
11	12	13	14	15	16	17
18	19	20	21	22	23	24
25	26	27	28	29	30	

SEPTEMBER

MONDAY   ROSH HASHANAH
12

TUESDAY
13

WEDNESDAY
14

THURSDAY
15

FRIDAY
16

COLUMBINE by Mary Alice Sinton, Ponca City, Oklahoma and Dr. Eleanor Sinton, Aurora, Colorado. This is an original Hawaiian quilt designed and cut by Mary and appliqued and quilted by her mother-in-law, Eleanor. The columbine flower pattern is the state flower of Colorado. Displayed at Quilt Kansas, Wichita, Kansas.

SATURDAY
17

SUNDAY
18

SEPTEMBER						
S	M	T	W	T	F	S
				1	2	3
4	5	6	7	8	9	10
11	12	13	14	15	16	17
18	19	20	21	22	23	24
25	26	27	28	29	30	

SEPTEMBER

MONDAY
19

TUESDAY
20

WEDNESDAY   YOM KIPPUR
21

THURSDAY
22

FRIDAY
23

TRANQUILITY by Lillian J. Leonard, Indianapolis, Indiana. 78″ x 92″. A flying geese border encloses an enlarged curved 2-patch center. The swag border defines the large areas of fine hand quilting. It was a winner in the Indianapolis Star/Block Contest. This quilt is now a permanent part of the AQS collection.

SATURDAY
24

SUNDAY
25

SEPTEMBER

S	M	T	W	T	F	S
				1	2	3
4	5	6	7	8	9	10
11	12	13	14	15	16	17
18	19	20	21	22	23	24
25	26	27	28	29	30	

SEPTEMBER / OCTOBER

MONDAY
26

TUESDAY
27

WEDNESDAY
28

THURSDAY
29

FRIDAY
30

CARPENTER'S WHEEL by Janet Myers, Fairbanks, Alaska. 77″ x 98″. Repositioning of the same group of fabrics gives diversity of interest to each block. Janet has hidden the quilt's name, date and initials in the hand quilted border. It was Grand Champion at the Alaska State Fair in Fairbanks.

SATURDAY
1

SUNDAY
2

OCTOBER						
S	M	T	W	T	F	S
						1
2	3	4	5	6	7	8
9	10	11	12	13	14	15
16	17	18	19	20	21	22
23	24	25	26	27	28	29
30	31					

OCTOBER

MONDAY

3

TUESDAY

4

WEDNESDAY

5

THURSDAY

6

FRIDAY

7

MARINER'S SUNSET by Shirley O'Meara, Hudson, New Hampshire. 37″ x 37″. Traditional designs used in an original setting create this medallion look. Hand appliqued and pieced except for the tall ships. It was shown at the New England Images II.

SATURDAY

8

SUNDAY

9

OCTOBER

S	M	T	W	T	F	S
						1
2	3	4	5	6	7	8
9	10	11	12	13	14	15
16	17	18	19	20	21	22
23	24	25	26	27	28	29
30	31					

OCTOBER

MONDAY   COLUMBUS DAY
10

TUESDAY
11

WEDNESDAY
12

THURSDAY
13

FRIDAY
14

THE WITHROW QUILT
by Rita Shimota, Hugo,
Minnesota. 84″ x 96″. Old
buildings in the small
disappearing community of
Withrow are reproduced in
applique on this quilt. It
was a winner at the
Minnesota State Fair.

SATURDAY
15

SUNDAY
16

OCTOBER

S	M	T	W	T	F	S
						1
2	3	4	5	6	7	8
9	10	11	12	13	14	15
16	17	18	19	20	21	22
23	24	25	26	27	28	29
30	31					

OCTOBER

MONDAY
17

TUESDAY
18

WEDNESDAY
19

THURSDAY
20

FRIDAY
21

PICKLE DISH by Bonnie Bus, Haslett, Michigan. This quilt is Bonnie's contemporary interpretation of a traditional pattern. She doubled the original block size and used an innovative setting. The rose and leaf quilting designs helped it win First Place at the Great Lakes Biannual Show in Mt. Clemons, Michigan.

SATURDAY
22

SUNDAY
23

OCTOBER

S	M	T	W	T	F	S
						1
2	3	4	5	6	7	8
9	10	11	12	13	14	15
16	17	18	19	20	21	22
23	24	25	26	27	28	29
30	31					

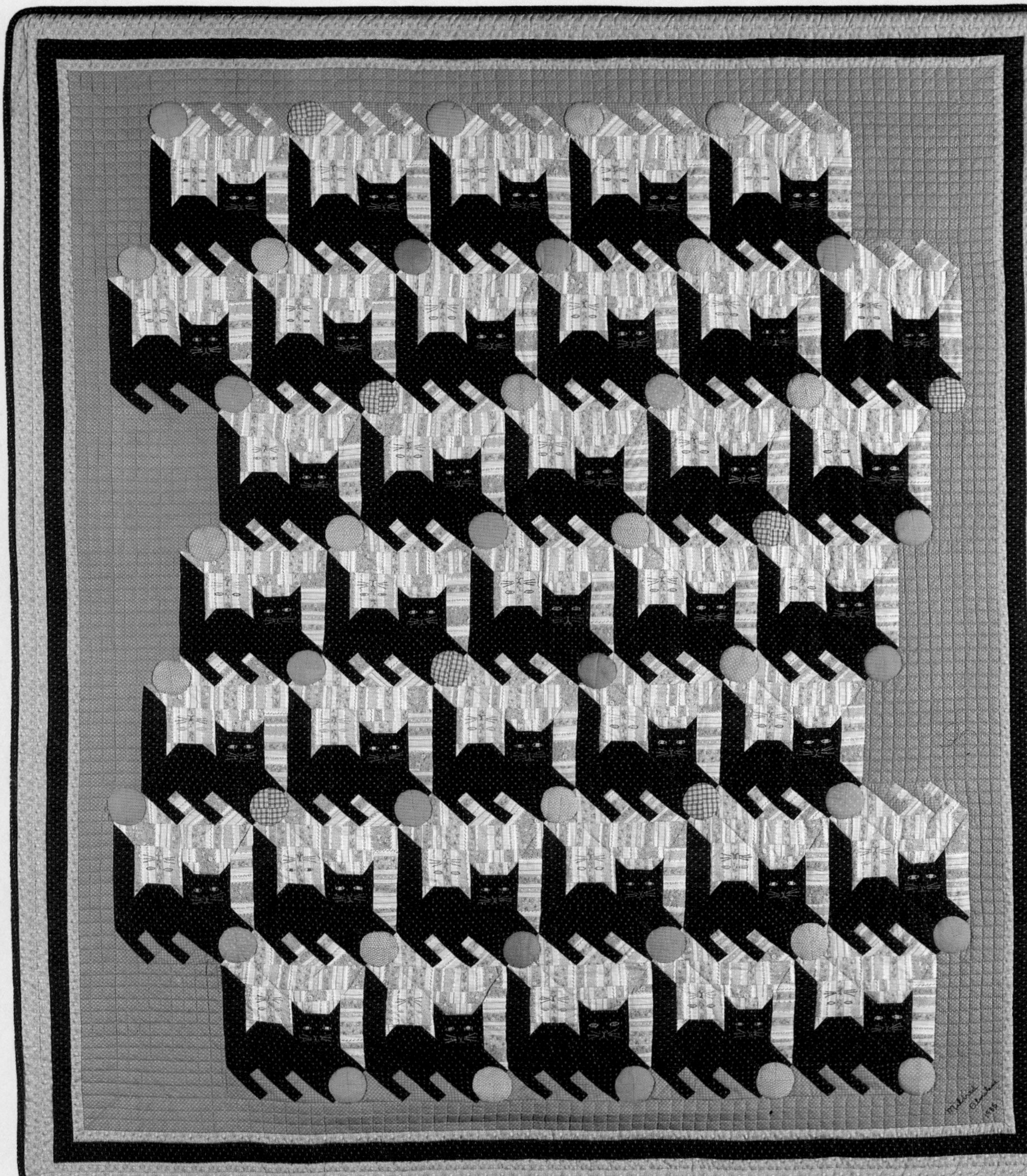

OCTOBER

MONDAY
24

TUESDAY
25

WEDNESDAY
26

THURSDAY
27

FRIDAY
28

COZY COUNTRY CATS by Mildred P. Olmstead, Hyrum, Utah. 84″ x 95″. 1,258 pieces were used in the 74 cat blocks of this Dawn Navarro design. This quilt was invited to hang at the Crossroads of the West, Salt Lake City, Utah and West Coast Quilter's Conference IX, Eugene, Oregon. To find the other delightful cats, turn this page upside down!

SATURDAY
29

SUNDAY
30

OCTOBER

S	M	T	W	T	F	S
						1
2	3	4	5	6	7	8
9	10	11	12	13	14	15
16	17	18	19	20	21	22
23	24	25	26	27	28	29
30	31					

OCTOBER / NOVEMBER

MONDAY   HALLOWEEN
31

TUESDAY
1

WEDNESDAY
2

THURSDAY
3

FRIDAY
4

KACHINA by Carol Meyer, Albuquerque, New Mexico. 45″ x 32″. This piece has been exhibited at the University of New Mexico, Cabrillo College in California and the northern New Mexico Quilt Guild Show in Santa Fe. Kachina dolls are made and used by the Hopi Indians of the Southwestern United States and represent the spirit of birds, animals, insects, plants and people.

SATURDAY
5

SUNDAY
6

			NOVEMBER			
S	M	T	W	T	F	S
		1	2	3	4	5
6	7	8	9	10	11	12
13	14	15	16	17	18	19
20	21	22	23	24	25	26
27	28	29	30			

NOVEMBER

MONDAY

7

TUESDAY   **ELECTION DAY**

8

WEDNESDAY

9

THURSDAY

10

FRIDAY   **VETERAN'S DAY**

11

EARLY NOVEMBER by Kathleen Weinheimer, Bridgewater, MA. 44″ x 44″. The last of the maples gives a certain yellow and pink cast to the earth in late fall that Kathleen has captured in this glowing piece. It has been displayed at the Plymouth County Cranberry Quilt Show, Carver, Massachusetts, and Quilts 86 at the Bridgewater Public Library.

SATURDAY

12

SUNDAY

13

NOVEMBER						
S	M	T	W	T	F	S
		1	2	3	4	5
6	7	8	9	10	11	12
13	14	15	16	17	18	19
20	21	22	23	24	25	26
27	28	29	30			

NOVEMBER

MONDAY
14

TUESDAY
15

WEDNESDAY
16

THURSDAY
17

FRIDAY
18

DOUBLE WEDDING RING MEDALLION by I.Q.'s Club, Speedway, Indiana. Duplicate quilting patterns on the solid blue set off this traditional pieced pattern. Displayed at NQA in Decatur, Illinois. The nine quilters who created this quilt have been a team since 1979.

SATURDAY
19

SUNDAY
20

NOVEMBER

S	M	T	W	T	F	S
		1	2	3	4	5
6	7	8	9	10	11	12
13	14	15	16	17	18	19
20	21	22	23	24	25	26
27	28	29	30			

NOVEMBER

MONDAY
21

TUESDAY
22

WEDNESDAY
23

THURSDAY   THANKSGIVING DAY
24

FRIDAY
25

CONNECTICUT "350" by Sandra E. Smith, Killingworth, Connecticut. 72″ x 72″. Commemorating Connecticut's 350th Birthday, this quilt is based on the Connecticut patchwork pattern with the "Charter Oak" in the center. The oak leaves border represents the 169 towns and cities in the state. This quilt won Best of Show at Somers, New York.

SATURDAY
26

SUNDAY
27

NOVEMBER
S	M	T	W	T	F	S
		1	2	3	4	5
6	7	8	9	10	11	12
13	14	15	16	17	18	19
20	21	22	23	24	25	26
27	28	29	30			

NOVEMBER / DECEMBER

MONDAY

28

TUESDAY

29

WEDNESDAY

30

THURSDAY

1

FRIDAY

2

THE LIBRARY by Judy Tescher, Pendleton, Indiana. 60″ x 70″. This original design was made from fabrics which were overdyed with household dye. It won First Place in the Professional Arts and Crafts Division at the Indiana State Fair and was displayed at Historic Centerville Indiana Show, where Judy was the featured quilter.

SATURDAY

3

SUNDAY   HANUKAH

4

DECEMBER

S	M	T	W	T	F	S
				1	2	3
4	5	6	7	8	9	10
11	12	13	14	15	16	17
18	19	20	21	22	23	24
25	26	27	28	29	30	31

DECEMBER

MONDAY

5

TUESDAY

6

WEDNESDAY   PEARL HARBOR DAY

7

THURSDAY

8

FRIDAY

9

STAINED GLASS by
Barbara Guzan, Ambridge,
Pennsylvania. Piecing the
black strips between the
"stained glass" sections
instead of appliqueing them
is Barbara's unique method
of construction. This quilt
was included in the
Keystone Quilt Show and
at the Wilmington,
Pennsylvania Show.

SATURDAY

10

SUNDAY

11

DECEMBER
S	M	T	W	T	F	S
				1	2	3
4	5	6	7	8	9	10
11	12	13	14	15	16	17
18	19	20	21	22	23	24
25	26	27	28	29	30	31

DECEMBER

MONDAY
12

TUESDAY
13

WEDNESDAY
14

THURSDAY
15

FRIDAY
16

FINE FEATHERED FRIENDS by Carol Doak, Windham, New Hampshire. 86″ x 86″. Hand pieced and hand quilted, this quilt features feathered stars and feathered quilting as a Christmas Quilt. Displayed at New England Images II and a winner of three blue ribbons at the Vermont Quilt Festival.

SATURDAY
17

SUNDAY
18

DECEMBER						
S	M	T	W	T	F	S
				1	2	3
4	5	6	7	8	9	10
11	12	13	14	15	16	17
18	19	20	21	22	23	24
25	26	27	28	29	30	31

DECEMBER

MONDAY
19

TUESDAY
20

WEDNESDAY
21

THURSDAY
22

FRIDAY
23

O CHRISTMAS TREE by Jane Harnden, Edmond, Oklahoma. 82″ x 96″. Music, an important part of Jane's family's Christmas tradition, led to the design of this second in a series of four quilts. It won Best of Show at the Oklahoma State Fair and was displayed at the American International Quilt Festival in Houston, Texas.

SATURDAY
24

SUNDAY   **CHRISTMAS DAY**
25

DECEMBER						
S	M	T	W	T	F	S
					1	2	3
4	5	6	7	8	9	10
11	12	13	14	15	16	17
18	19	20	21	22	23	24
25	26	27	28	29	30	31

DECEMBER / JANUARY

MONDAY
26

TUESDAY
27

WEDNESDAY
28

THURSDAY
29

FRIDAY
30

QUILTER'S DAYDREAM: STAR OF FEATHERS by Kathleen N. Herman, Cedar Falls, Iowa. 40″ x 40″. This quilt was one of two fiber pieces selected for the Northeast Iowa Competitive Art Show. The heavily stippled center provides a focus for the combination of Blazing Star and Kaleidoscope blocks. It was a first place winner in the Iowa Quilter's Guild Show.

SATURDAY
31

SUNDAY   **NEW YEAR'S DAY**
1

JANUARY

S	M	T	W	T	F	S
1	2	3	4	5	6	7
8	9	10	11	12	13	14
15	16	17	18	19	20	21
22	23	24	25	26	27	28
29	30	31				

1988

JANUARY	FEBRUARY	MARCH	APRIL
S M T W T F S	S M T W T F S	S M T W T F S	S M T W T F S
1 2	1 2 3 4 5 6	1 2 3 4 5	1 2
3 4 5 6 7 8 9	7 8 9 10 11 12 13	6 7 8 9 10 11 12	3 4 5 6 7 8 9
10 11 12 13 14 15 16	14 15 16 17 18 19 20	13 14 15 16 17 18 19	10 11 12 13 14 15 16
17 18 19 20 21 22 23	21 22 23 24 25 26 27	20 21 22 23 24 25 26	17 18 19 20 21 22 23
24 25 26 27 28 29 30	28 29	27 28 29 30 31	24 25 26 27 28 29 30
31			

MAY	JUNE	JULY	AUGUST
S M T W T F S	S M T W T F S	S M T W T F S	S M T W T F S
1 2 3 4 5 6 7	1 2 3 4	1 2	1 2 3 4 5 6
8 9 10 11 12 13 14	5 6 7 8 9 10 11	3 4 5 6 7 8 9	7 8 9 10 11 12 13
15 16 17 18 19 20 21	12 13 14 15 16 17 18	10 11 12 13 14 15 16	14 15 16 17 18 19 20
22 23 24 25 26 27 28	19 20 21 22 23 24 25	17 18 19 20 21 22 23	21 22 23 24 25 26 27
29 30 31	26 27 28 29 30	24 25 26 27 28 29 30	28 29 30 31
		31	

SEPTEMBER	OCTOBER	NOVEMBER	DECEMBER
S M T W T F S	S M T W T F S	S M T W T F S	S M T W T F S
1 2 3	1	1 2 3 4 5	1 2 3
4 5 6 7 8 9 10	2 3 4 5 6 7 8	6 7 8 9 10 11 12	4 5 6 7 8 9 10
11 12 13 14 15 16 17	9 10 11 12 13 14 15	13 14 15 16 17 18 19	11 12 13 14 15 16 17
18 19 20 21 22 23 24	16 17 18 19 20 21 22	20 21 22 23 24 25 26	18 19 20 21 22 23 24
25 26 27 28 29 30	23 24 25 26 27 28 29	27 28 29 30	25 26 27 28 29 30 31
	30 31		

1989

JANUARY	FEBRUARY	MARCH	APRIL
S M T W T F S	S M T W T F S	S M T W T F S	S M T W T F S
1 2 3 4 5 6 7	1 2 3 4	1 2 3 4	1
8 9 10 11 12 13 14	5 6 7 8 9 10 11	5 6 7 8 9 10 11	2 3 4 5 6 7 8
15 16 17 18 19 20 21	12 13 14 15 16 17 18	12 13 14 15 16 17 18	9 10 11 12 13 14 15
22 23 24 25 26 27 28	19 20 21 22 23 24 25	19 20 21 22 23 24 25	16 17 18 19 20 21 22
29 30 31	26 27 28	26 27 28 29 30 31	23 24 25 26 27 28 29
			30

MAY	JUNE	JULY	AUGUST
S M T W T F S	S M T W T F S	S M T W T F S	S M T W T F S
1 2 3 4 5 6	1 2 3	1	1 2 3 4 5
7 8 9 10 11 12 13	4 5 6 7 8 9 10	2 3 4 5 6 7 8	6 7 8 9 10 11 12
14 15 16 17 18 19 20	11 12 13 14 15 16 17	9 10 11 12 13 14 15	13 14 15 16 17 18 19
21 22 23 24 25 26 27	18 19 20 21 22 23 24	16 17 18 19 20 21 22	20 21 22 23 24 25 26
28 29 30 31	25 26 27 28 29 30	23 24 25 26 27 28 29	27 28 29 30 31
		30 31	

SEPTEMBER	OCTOBER	NOVEMBER	DECEMBER
S M T W T F S	S M T W T F S	S M T W T F S	S M T W T F S
1 2	1 2 3 4 5 6 7	1 2 3 4	1 2
3 4 5 6 7 8 9	8 9 10 11 12 13 14	5 6 7 8 9 10 11	3 4 5 6 7 8 9
10 11 12 13 14 15 16	15 16 17 18 19 20 21	12 13 14 15 16 17 18	10 11 12 13 14 15 16
17 18 19 20 21 22 23	22 23 24 25 26 27 28	19 20 21 22 23 24 25	17 18 19 20 21 22 23
24 25 26 27 28 29 30	29 30 31	26 27 28 29 30	24 25 26 27 28 29 30
			31

The American Quilter's Society

More than 20,000 quilters and quilt lovers already know about the benefits of being a member of the American Quilter's Society. Each member receives 4 issues a year of the magazine, *American Quilter*, which features informative and timely articles on quilting, along with full-color photographs of all kinds of quilts. Each member also receives her own attractive membership pin and card. The card allows free admission into the AQS annual show and contest in Paducah, Kentucky. In that show, the best quilts in the country are on exhibit under one roof. More than $30,000.00 is awarded in cash prizes to the contest-winning quilters each year. During the show, workshops and lectures are available. There is also an AQS fashion show and contest.

There are more benefits! Each member can purchase many of the best and latest quilting books at special discount prices. Members periodically receive the newsletter *Update* to keep up on the latest Society news. Members may sell quilts through the AQS Quilts For Sale catalog service. The Society is also establishing a contemporary quilt museum in Kentucky.

If you are interested in becoming an AQS member, send in the coupon below along with your membership fee. Four issues of *American Quilter* magazine alone are worth more than the cost of membership!

☐ **YES**, I want to become a **MEMBER** of the American Quilter's Society.

☐ (#2501) 1 yr. membership - $15.00   ☐ (#2502) 2 yr. membership - $27.00 ($3.00 savings)

☐ (#2503) 3 yr. membership - $40.00 ($5.00 savings)

Add $5.00 per year for foreign postage and handling.

Name_____

Address_____

City _____ State_____Zip_____

METHOD OF PAYMENT

☐ Check   ☐ Bill Me   Charge my: ☐ VISA   ☐ MasterCard

Cardholder's name_____

Card number _____

MC Interbank No._____Exp. date_____

Signature _____

American Quilter's Society

P.O. Box 3290 • Paducah, Kentucky 42001